MEMO-RANDOM

THIS BOOK OF **Lists, MEMORIES,** *and* MISCELLANY

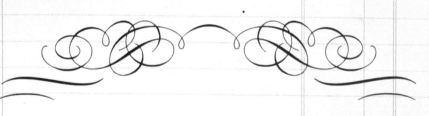

BELONGS TO:

{PASTE A PHOTOGRAPH OF YOUR DRIVER'S LICENSE OR PICTURE ID HERE}

A RANDOM MEMO

(ABOUT YOU)

YOU MIGHT WRITE IN THIS BOOK ONCE A YEAR OR FILL OUT THE WHOLE THING IN ONE AFTERNOON.

You can start on any page. Begin at the beginning or begin at the end, or randomly choose any page in between.

Any way you choose, you are creating a personal artifact—an artful miscellany of fact and memories, an accumulation of the bits and pieces of you.

32788N

Writing in this journal is supposed to feel like going through a box of ticket stubs, post-it doodles, and napkin scrawls. It's a scrappy, slaphappy way to make note of the little things that matter to you. It will contain stuff that you don't want to throw away or forget—and perhaps things that you'd like someone else discover one day.

You don't need to bare your soul in this journal. Sometimes, just emptying your pockets is revealing enough.

FAMILY TREE

FATHER FIGURE: Describe or **LIST THE WAYS THAT YOU'RE LIKE YOUR DAD.** Try thinking of everything from physical characteristics to personality traits to habits (good & bad).

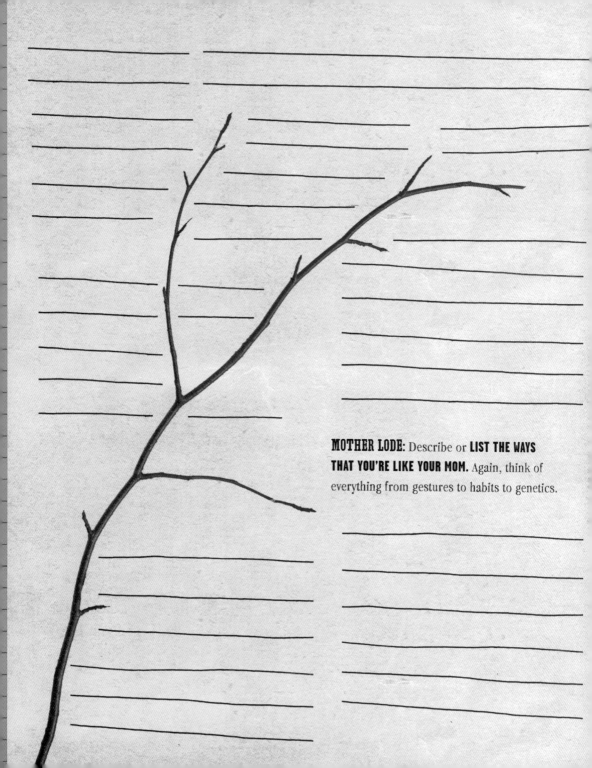

MOTHER LODE: Describe or **LIST THE WAYS THAT YOU'RE LIKE YOUR MOM.** Again, think of everything from gestures to habits to genetics.

Cinema Verité

Suppose that a **MOVIE IS GOING TO BE MADE OF YOUR LIFE.** List the major characters in this film (family, friends, partner, coworkers, etc.) and the **HOLLYWOOD ACTORS** who would play these roles.

931239

931239

810992

810992

Who would you
CAST TO PLAY YOURSELF?

TAKE STOCK

List everything that you had to **EAT AND DRINK** today.

Kiss *and* Tell

WRITE DOWN ALL OF THE
PEOPLE YOU'VE KISSED

(in the romantic way). Mark an asterisk
next to the top three kissers of all time.

THERE'S NO PLACE LIKE ♡ HOME ♡

List all of the
PLACES YOU'VE LIVED
(not just the towns or cities,
but every house or apartment
you've ever lived in). Put an
asterisk next to the best places.

List all the **PEOPLE YOU'VE LIVED WITH.**

List all of the **ANIMALS YOU'VE LIVED WITH.**

KEEP YOUR
FRIENDS CLOSE . . .

List the friends you've know the **LONGEST** (and how many years you've known them so far).

_____

_____

_____

_____

_____

_____

_____

_____

_____

_____

_____

_____

_____

_____

_____

_____

AND YOUR ENEMIES CLOSER

List your **FRENEMIES** (also known as "archrivals") from your past and present. If you don't have any relationships like this, list the friends you've lost over the years.

TAKE STOCK

List everything that you have **IN YOUR REFRIGERATOR** at the moment.

Dreamscapes

DO YOU HAVE ANY RECURRING DREAMS? Think of any themes, objects, people, or scenarios that appear repeatedly in your sleep. If you can't think of any, save this page to write about one dream as soon as you wake up.

RISKY
BUSINESS

List the **TOP FIVE SCARIEST,** potentially life-or-death **situations** you've been in.

1.

2.

3.

4.

5.

COWARDLY LION

List the things that **SCARE YOU THE MOST.**

Now write down **3 FEARS** you've overcome.

PLAYLISTS

A Your favorite **ROAD TRIP** music

B Songs that get you out on the **DANCE FLOOR**

A Your **FAVORITE** songs/bands of all time

B Songs/bands that you simply **CAN'T TOLERATE**

FE 90

FE

A Songs/bands that you have **PLAYED OUT**

B Music you listen to when you're **FEELING CRAPPY**

A The most **TRUTHFUL** songs about **LOVE**

B The best **BREAK-UP** tunes

WORD UP

List the words, slang, and **EXPRESSIONS** that you think are **OVERUSED.**

GIVE ME AN *adjective*

Fill this page with **WORDS** that you would like people to use to **DESCRIBE YOU.**

TAKE STOCK

List **EVERYTHING** you currently have **IN YOUR BAG OR PURSE.**

ADD IT TO THE COLLECTION

LIST THE THINGS YOU COLLECT
(or the things you'd like to collect if
you had enough space, time & funds).

Cinemagic

List your top ten all-time FAVORITE SCENES in the movies.

1

2

3

4

5

6

7

8

9

10

List the LAST FOUR MOVIES you saw.

1

2

3

4

NAME GAME

List ALL OF THE NAMES THAT YOU LOVE.
(These don't have to be names you would give to a child. They can even be names that you wish were yours).

HELLO
my name is

LIKE PEANUT BUTTER.

1 _____

2 _____

3 _____

4 _____

5 _____

6 _____

7 _____

8 _____

9 _____

10 _____

11 _____

12 _____

CLOSE THIS BOOK TO MAKE ONE BIG "FAVORITE COMBO" SANDWICH.

& JELLY

Some things are just **MEANT TO BE TOGETHER.** List the things you think make a **DYNAMIC DUO** (they don't all have to be food related).

1 _____

2 _____

3 _____

4 _____

5 _____

6 _____

7 _____

8 _____

9 _____

10 _____

11 _____

12 _____

CLOTHES
ENCOUNTERS
List your favorite pieces of clothing.

COLOR THEORY

FILL THESE SQUARES WITH YOUR FAVORITE COLORS (OR ATTACH PAINT CHIPS FROM A HARDWARE STORE).

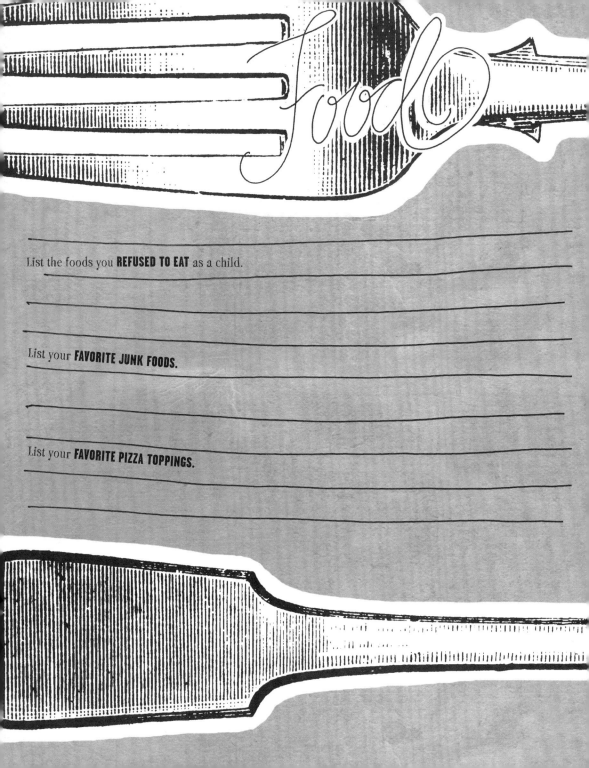

List the foods you **REFUSED TO EAT** as a child.

List your **FAVORITE JUNK FOODS.**

List your **FAVORITE PIZZA TOPPINGS.**

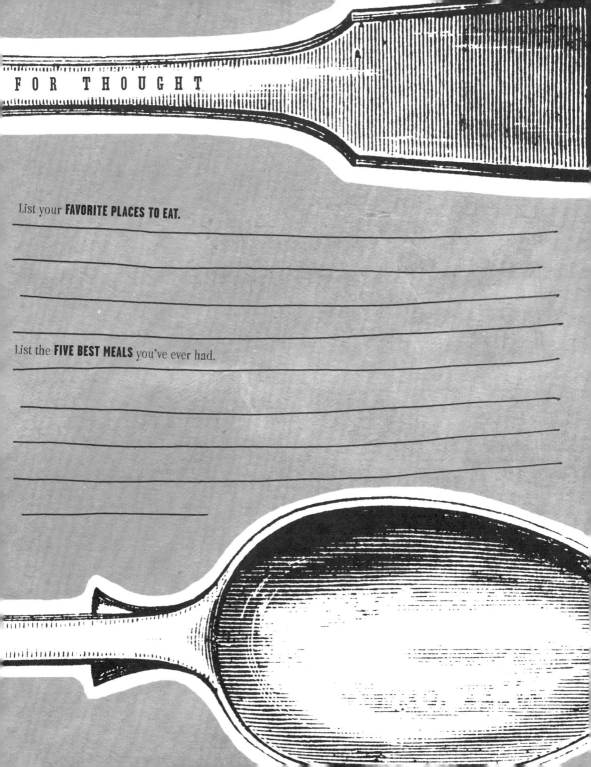

List your **FAVORITE PLACES TO EAT.**

List the **FIVE BEST MEALS** you've ever had.

CRUSH me

List all the **CRUSHES** you've ever had (celebrities, strangers, schoolmates, friends, and acquaintances).

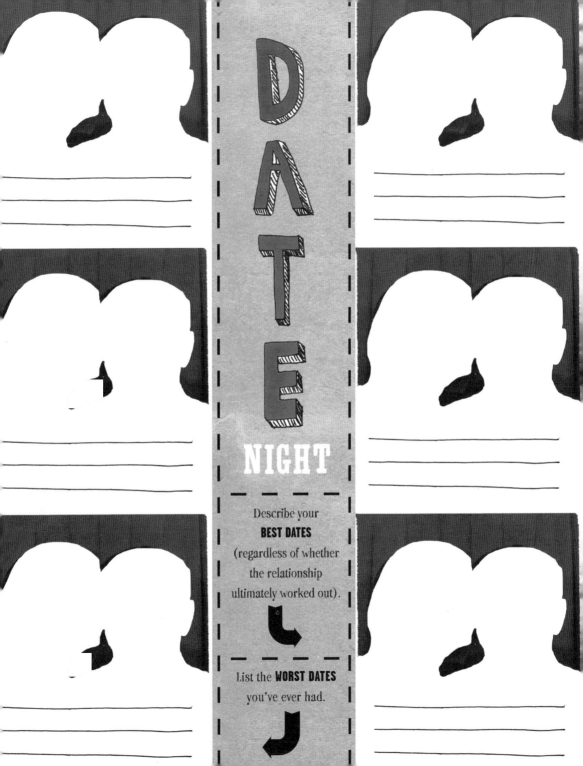

DATE

NIGHT

Describe your
BEST DATES
(regardless of whether
the relationship
ultimately worked out).

List the **WORST DATES**
you've ever had.

OH, THE PLACES YOU'LL GO

List all of the **PLACES YOU WANT TO GO BEFORE YOU DIE.** Go big, as if money, time, or technology weren't an issue.

CITY OF YOUR OWN

List all of the **CITIES** where you could **PICTURE YOURSELF LIVING.**

MINNESOTA

WISCONSIN

MICHIGAN

MAINE

VERMONT

NEW HAMPSHIRE

NEW YORK

MASSACHUSETTS

CONN.

RHODE ISLAND

IOWA

ILLINOIS

INDIANA

OHIO

PENNSYLVANIA

NEW JERSEY

DELAWARE

MARYLAND

MISSOURI

KENTUCKY

WEST VIRGINIA

VIRGINIA

ARKANSAS

TENNESSEE

NORTH CAROLINA

SOUTH CAROLINA

MISSISSIPPI

GEORGIA

ALABAMA

LOUISIANA

FLORIDA

MATTERS OF STATE

Color in all of the **STATES THAT YOU'VE VISITED**
(decide for yourself if an airport layover counts).

TAKE STOCK

What did you **DO THIS PAST WEEKEND?**

TAKING CARE OF BUSINESS

List the things you're **ANAL** about.

SPOOKY OR KOOKY?

List everything that you've ever been for **HALLOWEEN**.

_____

_____

_____

_____

_____

_____

_____

_____

_____

_____

_____

_____

_____

_____

DARK PLACES

Describe the **REASONS WHY PEOPLE MIGHT SEE YOU AS A LITTLE DARK**. Something in your sense of humor? Your taste in music? All that black eye makeup?

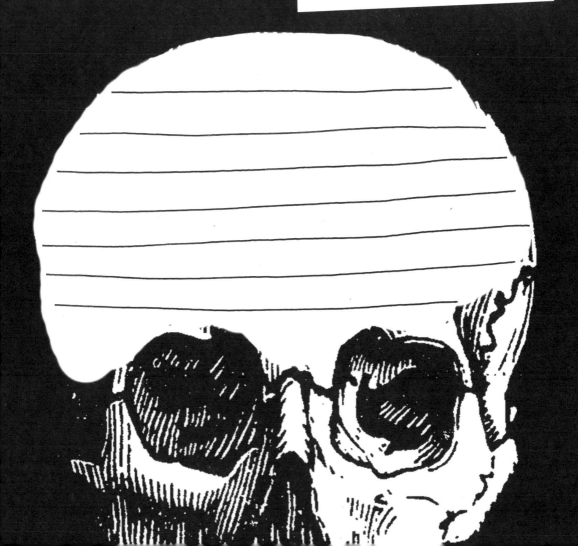

List all the **JOBS YOU'VE HAD** (put an asterisk next to your favorite ones).

JOB BOARD

List other **JOBS/CAREERS** that you're **INTERESTED** in.

List your **FAVORITE PEOPLE** you've **WORKED WITH.**

List the **STRANGEST PEOPLE**
you've **WORKED WITH.**

$PEND THRIFT

List the **EXPENSES** that—in your mind—
ARE COMPLETELY JUSTIFIED

	Promised Delivery Time		Date
	List the **LAST FIVE THINGS** you bought.		
1			
2			
3			
4			
5			
HANK YOU	Tax		
	Delivery		
0475	Total ▶		

Gift FOR THRIFT

List the **TEMPTATIONS** that you've learned to **RESIST.**

TAKE STOCK

List everything you're **WEARING RIGHT NOW.**

CERTIFICATE OF RECOGNITION

List all the **AWARDS YOU'VE WON** over your lifetime.

PERSONAL REACTIONS

List five people who make you **LAUGH** the most.

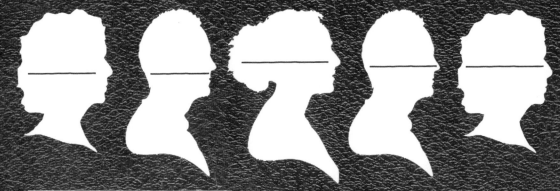

List five people who **PUSH YOUR BUTTONS.**

List five people (could be historical figures or your contemporaries) who **INSPIRE** you the most.

SORRY!

Sometimes it's hard to admit fault. List the people you think you **OWE AN APOLOGY TO.**

Now twist it. List the people you think **OWE YOU AN APOLOGY.**

Describe the **HARDEST APOLOGY** you've had to make.

MEDIA

List your **FAVORITE ONLINE DESTINATIONS** (blogs, websites, social networks).

List your **TOP TEN** all-time **FAVORITE AUTHORS** and/or books.

FRENZY

List the shows that you consider **"MUST-SEE TV."**

List your favorite **MAGAZINES AND NEWSPAPERS.**

List your favorite **RADIO STATIONS.**

ELEMENT OF
CHOICE

Awesome or tragic, list the
**10 BIGGEST, MOST MOMENTOUS
& IMPORTANT DECISIONS** you've
made. Don't think about the
outcome, just the choice.

72

67 73 87

IF ONLY...

List your **BIGGEST REGRETS**

List the people you wish **YOU'D MADE A PLAY FOR** (when you had the chance).

FIGHTIN' WORDS

List your **FAVORITE INSULTS,** or the most **CREATIVE INSULTS** you can think of.

GOSSIP PAGE

There must be a few people in your life who know where the bodies are buried. **LIST THE PEOPLE** who probably have the **MOST DIRT ON YOU.**

Have you ever done anything **SCANDALOUS** or **GOSSIP-WORTHY?**

List TEN THINGS THAT YOU'VE LOST over the course of your life
(you don't have to restrict the list to physical objects).

List the THINGS THAT YOU WOULD GRAB IF THE HOUSE WAS ON FIRE.

List some **THINGS YOU'VE FOUND** (again, they don't all have to be physical objects).

List **THREE ITEMS YOU'LL NEVER GIVE AWAY** or throw out.

AND FOUND

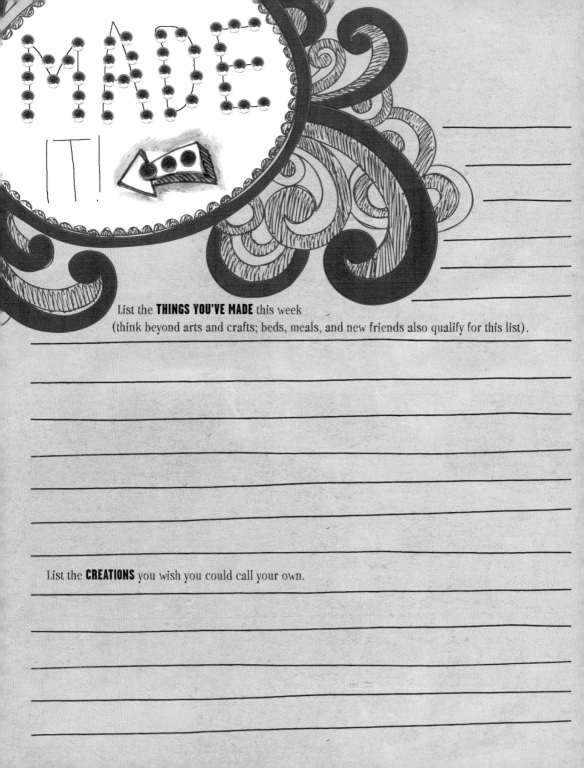

MADE IT!

List the **THINGS YOU'VE MADE** this week
(think beyond arts and crafts; beds, meals, and new friends also qualify for this list).

List the **CREATIONS** you wish you could call your own.

--SOUL MATE
SHOPPING LIST--

Maybe you've found the perfect mate, maybe
not. Make a list of words to describe your
soul mate. (If you don't believe in soul
mates, make a list of the characteristics
you'd like to have in a life-long partner.)

TROUBLE SPOTS

Ok, so maybe there are some areas where you got the **SHORT END OF THE STICK,** genetically speaking. List the features that you are less enthusiastic about.

HOT PROPERTY

**ALL MODESTY ASIDE,
LIST YOUR BEST FEATURES.**

SCHOOL DAYS

List your **BEST SUBJECTS** in school.

HIGHER LEARNING

Ignoring the price tag, time commitment, and other obstacles, list the **DEGREES YOU'D LOVE TO COLLECT** or **SUBJECTS THAT YOU'D WANT TO STUDY** some more.

TAKE STOCK

Look on your phone and list your **PAST 10 MISSED CALLS.**

List your **PAST 10 PLACED CALLS.**

List your **PAST 10 TEXT MESSAGES.**

If someone wanted to catch you, what could they use to **TEMPT YOU?** List the tangible or intangible things that someone could use to **LURE YOU INTO A TRAP.**

GOTCHA

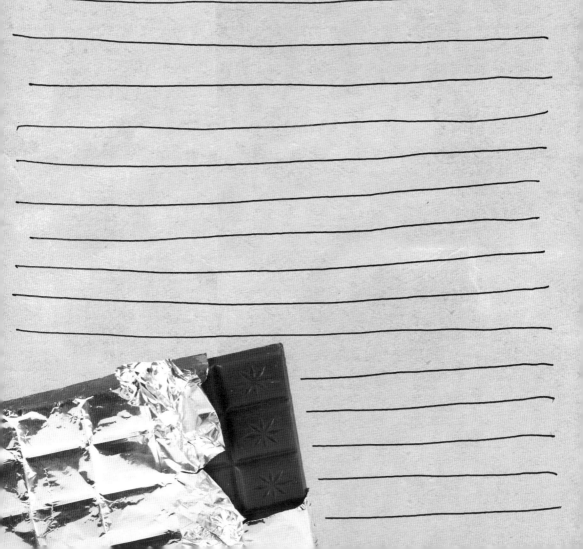

TAKE ME AWAY

{ from this Getaway }

Describe or list your **WORST TRAVELING EXPERIENCES** ever.

Paradise FOUND

LIST YOUR BEST VACATIONS, EVER.

GENUINE CURTEICH-CHICAGO "C.T. ART-COLORTONE" POST CARD (REG. U.S. PAT. OFF.)

POST CARD

PLACE
STAMP
HERE

_____

_____

_____

_____

_____

_____

16241

MADE IN U.S.A BY E.C. KROPP CO., MILWAUKEE, WIS. ————— (XXX)

POST CARD

PLACE
STAMP
HERE

_____

_____

_____

_____

_____

_____

_____

_____

_____

List the personality traits or **PHYSICAL FEATURES** that catch your attention.

List your **AUTOMATIC RED FLAGS** when it comes to getting involved with someone.

OFF

FIVE EASY PIECES

List 5 predictions
for yourself that
you think will
happen in the next
five years.

MORE

FIVE EASY PIECES

Ask a friend
to list five
predictions
for you.

Think of who you were five years ago. Now, **DESCRIBE FIVE THINGS THAT HAVE HAPPENED TO YOU IN THE PAST FIVE YEARS** that your self from five years ago would be shocked to find out.

_____

_____

_____

_____

_____

_____

_____

_____

_____

_____

_____

_____

_____

_____

_____

_____

_____

List five things you're **HAPPY YOU HAVE RIGHT NOW.**

List five things that you **WANT RIGHT NOW.**

WANT IT

LIST THE TOP FIVE TIMES YOU'VE BEEN THE SICKEST

— WHAT ARE THE BEST REMEDIES WHEN YOU FEEL ILL? —

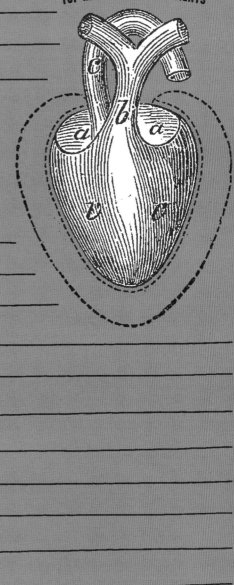

HEART TROUBLE

LIFE HURTS. WRITE DOWN YOUR
TOP HEARTBREAKING MOMENTS

PARTY TIME

LIST THE BEST PARTIES YOU'VE BEEN TO

ENTOURAGE

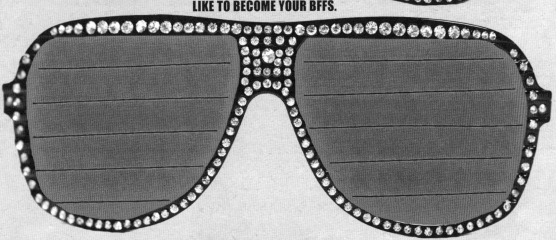

IF YOU SUDDENLY
BECAME FAMOUS,
LIST THE CELEBRITIES THAT YOU'D
LIKE TO BECOME YOUR BFFS.

FIGHT

CLUB

1. List the top five **BIGGEST ARGUMENTS** you've gotten into.

2. List the people you **FIGHT WITH THE MOST.**

3. List any **PHYSICAL FIGHTS** you've been in (and who won).

4. What things are **WORTH FIGHTING ABOUT?**

What's Eating You?

List five things that you are WORRIED ABOUT right this minute.

_____

_____

_____

_____

_____

_____

_____

_____

_____

Come back to this page in SIX MONTHS. Are any of these things still on your mind?

_____

_____

_____

_____

_____

_____

_____

_____

_____

Let It Be

There are lots of things in life to stress over; instead, list the things you're NOT WORRIED ABOUT.

_____

_____

_____

_____

_____

_____

_____

_____

_____

_____

_____

_____

_____

_____

_____

_____

_____

_____

_____

_____

_____

NATURAL GIFTS

List the things that **COME NATURALLY TO YOU.** Think of talents, activities, subjects, or situations. No? Go ask you're parents or friends. They can list them.

NOT IN YOUR NATURE

List the things that are a **STRUGGLE** for you.

TAKE STOCK

List all of the people **YOU'VE TALKED WITH** today.

TOY STORY

Think back to your childhood and list the **THINGS YOU COVETED AS A KID.**

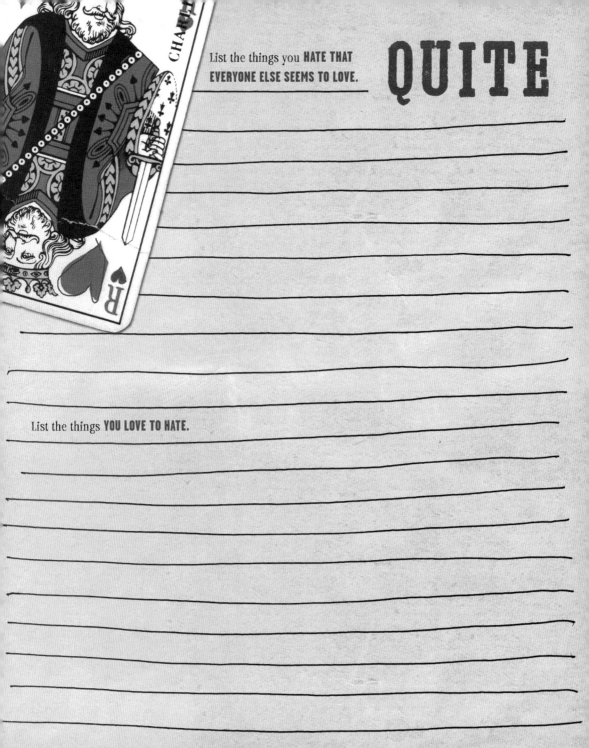

List the things you **HATE THAT EVERYONE ELSE SEEMS TO LOVE.**

QUITE

List the things **YOU LOVE TO HATE.**

CONTRARY

List the things you **SECRETLY LOVE,** but won't admit it.

_____

_____

_____

_____

_____

_____

_____

_____

_____

List the people or things that you **USED TO LOVE, BUT NOW HATE.**

_____

_____

_____

_____

_____

_____

_____

_____

UMM...YEAH...AWKWARD

List your most **EMBARRASSING** moments.

HELPING HAND

List your **BEST DEEDS**.

TAKE STOCK

List 10 things that **INTEREST YOU** at the moment

LIST ALL OF YOUR TATTOOS.

If you don't have any, list the ones
that you might consider getting,
and where they would go.

SCENT-SATIONAL

List all of your **FAVORITE SMELLS.**

Be -YOU- tiful

WHAT, IN YOUR OPINION, IS ODDLY BEAUTIFUL?

TO DO

Make a list of things **YOU HAVE TO DO . . .**

DONE

Make a list of **THINGS YOU'VE DONE . . .**

REST IN PEACE

List the things that you **HOPE PEOPLE WILL SAY ABOUT YOU** at your funeral.